TV LAMPS

IDENTIFICATION AND VALUE GUIDE

TOM SANTISO

COLLECTOR BOOKS

A Division of Schroeder Publishing Co., Inc.

The current values in this book should be used only as a guide. They are not intended to set prices, which vary from one section of the country to another. Auction prices as well as dealer prices vary greatly and are affected by condition as well as demand. Neither the author nor the publisher assumes responsibility for any losses that might be incurred as a result of consulting this guide.

Searching For A Publisher?

We are always looking for knowledgeable people considered to be experts within their fields. If you feel that there is a real need for a book on your collectible subject and have a large comprehensive collection, contact Collector Books.

Front cover: Deco horse, $85.00 – 100.00; Deco fawn with planter, $75.00 – 95.00; crouching panther, $75.00 – 100.00.
Back cover: Ceramic ship with lighted portholes, $75.00 – 80.00; large flying duck with planter, $100.00 – 125.00; Maddux of California swan with planter, $93.00 – 110.00.

Cover design by Beth Summers
Book design by Beth Ray

COLLECTOR BOOKS
P.O. Box 3009
Paducah, Kentucky 42002-3009

Copyright © 1999 Tom Santiso

Contents

Acknowledgments

All the lamps in this book are from my own collection. Without help from my friends, I would never have been able to accumulate such a large collection in so short a time. These folks always watched out for them at auctions, yard sales, and flea markets and were kind enough to buy them for me. To them I dedicate this book. My sincere thanks.

Pricing

Many factors affect the price of any antique, and so it is with TV lamps. These prices were arrived at from research done at auctions, yard sales, and shops, by conferring with antique dealers across the country, and comparing lamps and prices with other collectors.

The prices vary greatly in different parts of the country. Many lamps were made in California and the prices there are much higher. Also, in New York City and on the East Coast they seem to be higher. Of course, the condition, original flowers and parts figure greatly in prices. Lamps showing the Art Deco influence or ones signed by the artist-designer are more valuable.

After enjoying this book, I hope you will find the rapidly growing interest in TV lamps contagious. Up to now, TV lamps have only been included as part of books on lamps of the 1950s. I hope this book will raise them to their own level of interest and collecting. Happy hunting.

Introduction

Shortly after the arrival of television sets in the American home, along came the TV lamp. In the 1920s television was only experimental, and by 1941 it was ready for the commercial market. However the war and its need for certain materials kept regular production and programming from being fully developed. Between 1948 and 1958, TV was in its full glory. Because the early sets had small screens and rather dark pictures, it was feared that the extensive viewing in a dark room would cause eye damage. Yet too much direct light diminished the picture quality. Thus from the earlier radio lamps evolved the TV lamp. They feature a decorative form of an animal or other object with the bulb in back or inside; some also have a small shade.

From the advent, there was a virtual flurry of designs and materials used to make the lamps. Any person, bird, animal, or thing was fair game as a model for a TV lamp. The most common material used was ceramics, some of beautiful near-porcelain quality. Other lamps were made of plaster, chalk, glass, metal, or wood. Some doubled as planters, accompanied by plastic plants or a package of potting soil. The Art Deco influence is seen in some examples and many were exquisite forms and shapes. Even today people are fooled into thinking they have found a nice figure of a horse or ballerina, when in reality it is a TV lamp without the bulb fixture. If looked at carefully, in the back you will see a scooped-out place where a light fixture used to be.

The illustration at right shows a lamp back with a light fixture and another with the hole where the fixture was. The illustration at the right shows how the same mold was used for both a TV lamp and a regular lamp. Many times TV lamps were produced in two or more colors.

Not too much is known about the companies that made TV lamps because many are not marked. Those that are marked with the company or designer are indicated here with the photos. The most common companies were in California, many lamps just noting "Made in California, USA." The companies and designers represented in this book are Lane of Van Nuys, California, 1956 – 1966; Royal Haeger, Dundee, Illinois, Designer, Arden Hickman; Maddux, Los Angeles, California, 1937 – 1974; PGH Statuary; Phil-Mar Corporation, Cleveland, Ohio; Luminart; Kron, Designer from Texas; McCoy, Roseville, Ohio; Hallfield; L.M. Fielack; Williams China; Bilt-Rite; Esgo-Light Corporation; Metro Ware; Sheridan China; Puccini Novelty Art Company; American Statuary; Marcia of California; Buckingham; Duquesne; Royal China Novelty Company.

Birds and Other Winged Species

Miniature flying duck with planter signed: Lane Co., $65.00 – 95.00. With original plastic plants, $75.00 – 100.00.

Miniature flying duck with original plastic and paper plants, $85.00 – 95.00.

Large flying duck, 15",
with planter, $100.00
– 125.00.

Miniature flying duck with planter, brass holder,
$75.00 – 95.00.

Medium flying duck, 12", with planter, $75.00 – 90.00.

Medium flying duck, $75.00 – 90.00.

Ceramic flying duck with wooden base, $82.00 – 97.00.

Flying duck, $75.00 – 90.00.

Swan with planter, signed Maddux of California, $85.00 – 100.00. With original plastic plants, $93.00 – 110.00.

Swan with blue base and planter, signed Maddux of Calif., $95.00 – 110.00.

Flying duck with planter, $65.00 – 85.00.

Miniature swan, 8", $50.00 – 60.00.

Double swan; plaster with Fiberglas shade, signed M. Fielack, $110.00 – 125.00.

Swan with light inside, holes in wings light up, $80.00 – 95.00.

Swan with planter,
$65.00 – 90.00.

Large swan with light inside, base of large wing lights up, 18", $110.00 – 125.00.

Large 17" swan with light inside, $95.00 – 110.00.

Small swan with planter and Fiberglas shade, $55.00 – 70.00.

Porcelain-like exotic bird with planter, $85.00 – 100.00.

Porcelain-like owl, light-up eyes, signed Kron, $125.00 – 135.00.

Crowing rooster on fence, signed Lane, $95.00 – 110.00.

Blue/green rooster with rising sun, $125.00 – 140.00.

Rooster with light inside, $55.00 – 75.00.

Green rooster, 18",
$85.00 – 90.00.

Large bird with gold decoration, 16", $120.00 – 130.00.

Porcelain-like pair of doves, $65.00 – 95.00.

Double doves with original plastic flowers and gold decoration, $75.00 – 95.00.

Bisque double blue jay, $60.00 – 75.00.

Bisque double bluebird with planter, $75.00 – 90.00.

Cockatoo with brass base and planter, signed E21855M, $75.00 – 90.00.

Double egret with planter, $65.00 – 95.00.

Bisque parrot with planter, $85.00 – 100.00.

Blue jay pair with planter, $55.00 – 65.00.

Big Cats

Crouching panther with planter, red most rare, $65.00 – 95.00.

Two black panthers, $75.00 – 85.00.

Black panther with planter, $45.00 – 65.00.

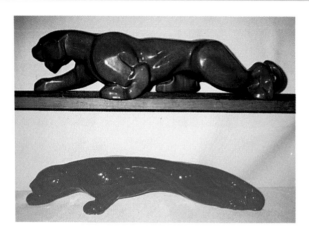

Crouching panther
in 6 colors, white
and green rare,
$75.00 – 100.00.

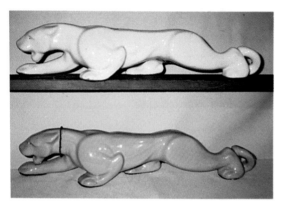

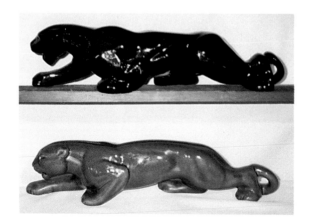

Black and green panthers with planters, $65.00 – 75.00.

Panther on rocks, $75.00 – 85.00.

Green panther with wire frames for original flowers, $55.00 – 65.00.

22K decorated panther with planter, signed Royal China Novelty Co., LeMieux China, $125.00 – 150.00.

Black panther with planter, $55.00 – 65.00.

Deco cheetah 17", $95.00 – 110.00.

Double panther, $75.00 – 95.00.

Panther with removable Fiberglas shade, $65.00 – 95.00.

Panther with two planters, $62.50 – 72.50.

Striding panther with planter, $75.00 – 90.00.

Large leopard with top metal planter, $125.00 – 145.00.

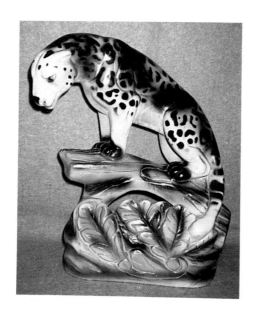

Large 14" plaster leopard, $200.00 – 225.00.

Plaster panther with Fiberglas shade, $75.00 – 90.00.

Black panther, plaster with Fiberglas shade, $85.00 – 95.00.

Black panther on rocks, $65.00 – 75.00.

Green panther on rocks, $60.00 – 65.00.

Tan and green panthers on rocks, $60.00 – 65.00.

Horses

Deco horse head with light inside, $75.00 – 95.00.

Large 16" ceramic horse head, $65.00 – 90.00.

Deco rearing horse, $110.00 – 125.00.

Wood base donkey with planter, signed Royal Haeger (label), $95.00 – 105.00.

Rearing horse with 22K gold decoration, $95.00 – 110.00.

Rearing horse with fence, signed California Original, USA, L-431, $85.00 – 112.00.

Rearing horse, $55.00 – 70.00.

Rearing horse with planter, $90.00 – 120.00.

Deco leaping horse with planter, $65.00 – 80.00; with original plastic flowers, $85.00 – 110.00.

Double Deco horse heads with planter, $85.00 –
100.00.

Bisque horses on ceramic background, $75.00 – 95.00.

Rearing horse with planter,
$65.00 – 80.00.

Porcelain prancing horse with light inside, holes above wall light up, $95.00 – 110.00.

Metal horses and wagon with clock and Fiberglas shade, bulb inside canopy, $110.00 – 125.00.

Deco horse, $85.00 – 100.00.

Double rearing horses, $70.00 – 90.00.

Double horse heads
with double planters,
$45.00 – 55.00.

Small donkey with original plastic flowers, $45.00 – 60.00.

Deco horse with planter, $70.00 – 90.00.

White leaping horse against fence, $75.00 – 85.00.

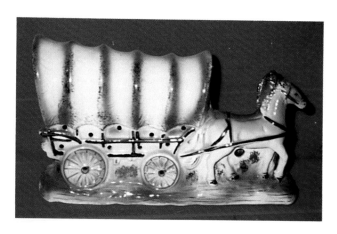

Small covered wagon and horses, 10", $45.00 – 60.00.

Prancing horse, $75.00
– 90.00.

Plaster Roman gladiator on chariot, Fiberglas shade, $220.00 – 250.00.

Near-porcelain ceramic horse, signed Lane, Van Nuys, CA, circa 1958, $95.00 – 110.00.

Porcelain type horse, signed Maddux of Calif., E21858M, $95.00 – 120.00.

Double horse with planter, gold decoration, $75.00 – 90.00.

Horse and colt, $85.00 – 90.00.

Metal horse and carriage with glass insert, $85.00 – 100.00.

White Deco horse with gold flecks and planter, $75.00 – 95.00.

Double rearing horses, $75.00 – 95.00.

Horse and colt with planter, $90.00 – 95.00.

Horse head with planter, $60.00 – 75.00.

Deco horse head, $60.00 – 65.00.

Ceramic horse with original paper flowers in wire frames, gold decorated, $110.00 – 135.00.

Pair of Deco horses, signed Royal Haeger (label), $125.00 – 150.00.

Black leaping horse, $85.00 – 110.00.

Prancing horse with planter, $90.00 – 120.00.

Deco horse head, $80.00 – 100.00.

Deco horse with paper shade and planter, signed Modern Art Products, Kansas City, MO, 1953, $110.00 – 135.00.

Tan horse head with light inside bottom of green wreath,
$100.00 – 120.00.

Ceramic donkey with planter, $65.00 – 80.00.

Oriental

Lady figure, $75.00 – 85.00.

Plaster Oriental figures with Fiberglas shade, $120.00 – 135.00.

Dragon vase, bulb inside, $55.00
– 70.00.

Chalkware chair with Fiberglas shade,
$75.00 – 85.00.

Oriental sampan with planter, holes light up, $75.00 – 95.00.

Plaster girl with Fiberglas back shade, $85.00 – 100.00.

Plaster figure with Fiberglas shade and gold decoration, $95.00 – 110.00.

Large 27" plaster Oriental boat with clamp-on Fiberglas shade, $150.00 – 195.00.

Plaster Oriental figures, removable figures and top, bulb inside well (all have basic differences in construction and color), $120.00 – 135.00.

Plaster Oriental lamp, signed Zini Pat., $95.00 – 110.00.

Sampan with two figures, windows light up, $65.00 – 90.00.

Green gondola with windows that light up, $85.00 – 90.00.

Black sampan with two figures, windows light up, $65.00 – 90.00.

Sampan with two figures, bulb inside that lights up windows, signed Premco Mfg. Co., Chicago, Ill. 1954, $65.00 – 90.00.

White metal Oriental figures, $75.00 – 100.00.

Plaster gondola with Fiberglas shade, $75.00 – 80.00.

Plaster gondola with Fiberglas shade, $65.00 – 80.00.

Plaster gondola with plastic removable shade (lifts), $85.00 – 90.00.

Ships

Wooden ship with paper sails, $65.00 – 90.00.

Plaster ship, port-
holes light up, $80.00
– 95.00

Plaster ship with reverse painting on glass background, signed Duquesne Statuary, $125.00 – 130.00.

All plaster ship with hand painted body, $75.00 – 95.00.

Small 12" ship,
$45.00 – 55.00.

Golden ship, pot metal, portholes light up, $85.00 – 95.00.

Small ceramic ship with brass footed base, signed Made in Calif., #3500-5321855, $60.00 – 85.00.

Airbrushed decorated ship, $65.00 – 80.00.

Ceramic paddle boat with planter, $70.00 – 90.00.

Metal ship with missing glass back shade, $65.00 – 90.00.

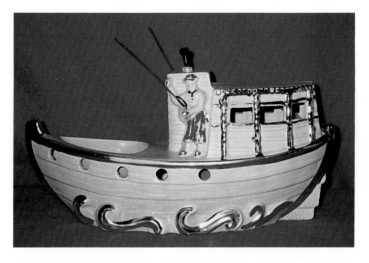

Pink fishing boat with metal poles and lighted windows, $95.00 – 120.00.

Ceramic ship with metal sails, portholes light up, $75.00 – 80.00.

Ceramic ship with metal sails, port- holes light up, $75.00 – 90.00.

Small ceramic ship with planter, $40.00 – 45.00.

Ceramic ship with heavy gilt decoration, $95.00 – 110.00.

Ceramic ship with metal sails, portholes light up,
$75.00 – 80.00.

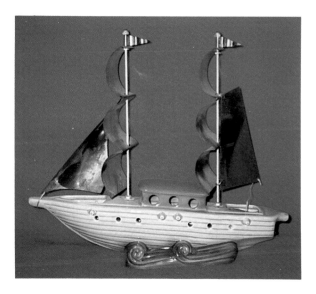

Ship with metal sails, portholes light up, $75.00 – 80.00.

All metal ship, portholes light up, $75.00 – 90.00.

Ceramic ship with metal sails, portholes light up, $75.00 – 90.00.

Plaster ship with airbrushed decoration, $75.00 – 95.00.

Bisque, airbrushed Nordic ship, $75.00 – 90.00.

Small 6" ship with planter, $45.00 – 55.00.

Bisque sailing ship with gilt decoration, $75.00 – 90.00.

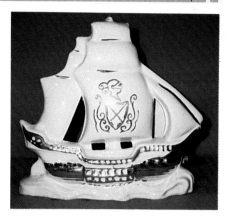

Ceramic ship in 3 colors, portholes light up, $65.00 –
85.00.

Ceramic ship (in 3 colors) with lighted portholes, $75.00 – 80.00.

Deer

Deer and fawn with planter, $75.00 – 85.00

Deco gazelle with planter, $75.00 – 95.00.

Near-porcelain deer, signed Maddux of Calif., Made in U.S.A., E21855M, $95.00 – 110.00.

Brown gazelle with planter, $70.00 – 95.00.

Leaping gazelle with planter, $70.00 – 90.00.

Standing stag,
$75.00 – 95.00.

Triple deer, Deco, with planter, $65.00 – 95.00.

Ceramic fawn, $65.00 – 85.00.

Double deer with planter, $70.00 – 85.00.

Deco gazelle with planter, $65.00 – 80.00.

Small 8" fawn with planter, $45.00 – 60.00.

Double gazelle with planter, $75.00 – 90.00.

Plaster "Dying Stag," airbrushed decoration, light inside flower, $100.00 – 135.00.

Deco deer and fawn, $95.00 – 110.00.

Double deco deer with Fiberglas shade, $110.00 – 125.00.

Deer and fawn, wooden base and Fiberglas shade, $75.00 – 90.00.

White metal cabin and deer with glass insert, $60.00 – 75.00.

Ceramic Deco gazelle, $85.00 – 95.00.

Deer and fawn heads with Fiberglas shade, $75.00 – 90.00.

Leaping deer with planter, $60.00 – 70.00.

Leaping deer, $55.00 – 65.00.

Deco gazelle with original flowers, $95.00 – 110.00.

Bisque double deer, signed E21855A, $65.00 – 90.00.

Deco fawn with planter, $75.00 – 95.00.

Deco deer with original glass flowers, $65.00 – 85.00.

Large 20" Deco gazelle, $95.00 – 110.00.

Plaster Deco gazelle with double bulbs inside tray, signed 124, $110.00 – 125.00.

Deco ceramic deer with planter, $55.00 – 75.00.

Plaster gazelle with planter and Fiberglas shade, $110.00 – 125.00

Dogs and Cats

Ceramic cats with eyes that light up, signed Kron, $95.00 – 110.00.

Cat and two kittens with glass eyes, signed 8511, $95.00 – 110.00.

Double Siamese cats with glass eyes, signed Lane & Co., Van Nuys, Calif. USA, $95.00 – 120.00.

Scotty dogs made of pressed paper, $75.00 – 95.00.

Bulldog with flock coating, eyes glow, $60.00 – 80.00.

Gray Scotty dog, $65.00 – 75.00.

Plaster Victorian lady with dog and Fiberglas shade, signed L.M. Fielack, $100.00 – 135.00.

Yorky dog, plaster, signed Rock-O-Stone, $75.00 – 85.00.

Plaster dogs on radio speaker that lights up, flocked coating, $65.00 – 90.00.

Plaster double dog, with Fiberglas shade, signed L.M. Fielack, $110.00 – 135.00.

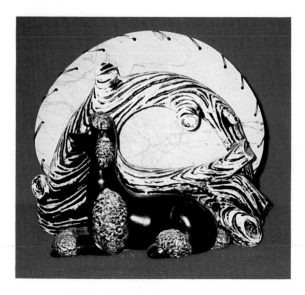

Deco black poodle, plaster with Fiberglas shade, signed C.M.A., $110.00 – 120.00.

Small 6" dog with light inside bowl, $45.00 – 55.00.

Plaster dog with ball that lights, $90.00 – 110.00.

Plaster dog with Fiberglas shade, $85.00 – 110.00.

Black greyhound, $70.00 – 95.00.

Double cats, near-porcelain quality, eyes light up, signed Kron, $125.00 – 150.00.

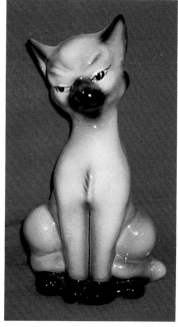

Ceramic cat, eyes light up, $75.00 – 100.00.

Double bulldog, eyes light up, signed Williams Ceramics, WH56 Claes, $120.00 – 135.00.

Double greyhounds, $72.50 – 85.00.

Plaster German shepherd with two candleholders and Fiberglas shade, $125.00 – 140.00.

Vehicles

Auto with planter, $45.00 – 50.00.

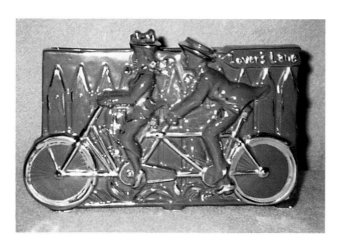

Two bicyclists with planter, signed Lover's Lane, $95.00 – 110.00.

Ceramic coach, $45.00 – 65.00.

Small 9" metal coach with Fiberglas shade, $65.00 – 95.00.

Plaster covered wagon with red paper shade, signed L. Pelle-
grini & Co., G72, $125.00 – 140.00.

Translucent porcelain-like covered wagon with light inside, signed Marcia of Calif., $95.00 – 110.00.

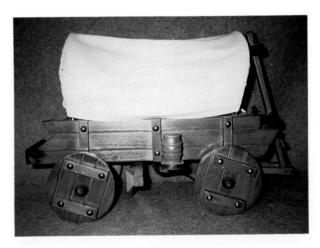

Wooden and cloth covered wagon, light inside, $65.00 – 90.00.

Balsa wood covered wagon with painted shade, light
inside, $75.00 – 95.00.

Ceramic wagon with light inside, $90.00 – 95.00.

Bisque coach with light inside, brass base, $100.00 – 110.00

Bisque 23" long coach and horses with light inside coach, brass base, $125.00 – 150.00.

People

Male ballet dancer, plaster with Fiberglas shade, signed American Statuary Co., $85.00 – 95.00.

Plaster ballerina with Fiberglas shade, $100.00 – 125.00.

Chalk girl with ducks, $75.00 – 100.00.

Plaster Jesus with Fiberglas back shade,
$120.00 – 150.00.

Porcelain sea nymph on shell, brass base, $85.00 – 100.00.

Plaster dancer on wood base with plastic shade, $75.00 – 95.00.

Clown head on white metal base, $65.00 – 95.00.

Plaster Victorian couple at grand piano, $120.00 – 135.00.

Ceramic dancer with gold fleck decoration, $55.00 – 75.00.

Plaster ballerina on bench with pin cup, Fiberglas shade, $120.00 – 135.00.

Ceramic ballet dancers, $85.00 – 95.00.

Ceramic mermaid with Fiberglas shade, $85.00 – 110.00.

Plaster oriental with blue speck decoration, Fiberglas shade, $110.00 – 135.00.

Pot metal figure with bulb inside ruby glass cup, $75.00 – 90.00.

Black man with pin holder, $135.00 – 150.00.

Plaster madonna and child, bulb lights up faces, $150.00 – 175.00.

Plaster madonna with child, bulb lights up faces, signed D.S.S., $150.00 – 175.00.

Bisque group with brass base, light inside carriage, $120.00 – 135.00.

Madonna with airbrushed decoration, $85.00 – 100.00.

Ceramic madonna, $45.00 – 55.00.

Plaster ballerina with Fiberglas shade, signed Puccini Art Novelty Co., $125.00 – 140.00.

Lady's head with light inside, $60.00 – 70.00.

Translucent porcelain head, bulb inside, $100.00 – 125.00.

Plaster harem girl with Fiberglas shade, $125.00 – 150.00.

Lady with greyhound, planter,
$110.00 – 120.00.

Plaster black man with removable clamped-on Fiberglas shade, $115.00 – 135.00.

Ceramic matador, signed Lane of California, $95.00 – 120.00.

Plaster nude, missing tall globe in back, $55.00 – 70.00; if complete, $85.00 – 100.00.

Ceramic matador and bull, $85.00 – 100.00.

Plaster Jesus with light inside, flowers light up face, $95.00 – 110.00.

Fancy dancer with planter and brass base, $80.00 – 95.00.

Plaster Victorian lady, $85.00 – 100.00.

Plaster Victorian lady with stenciled and hand painted dress, $100.00 – 125.00.

Fish and Animals

Green ceramic elephant with light inside, $65.00 – 90.00.

Large green elephant, $75.00 – 90.00.

Double fish with planter, $75.00 – 95.00.

Golden boy on dolphin, signed Lane and Co., Van Nuys, Calif.,
$95.00 – 105.00.

Swordfish with gold decoration, $75.00 – 95.00.

Ceramic fish with glass beads that light, $45.00 – 60.00.

Miniature squirrel, signed Lane Ceramics, #8528, $50.00 – 55.00.

Double ceramic fish, $75.00 – 95.00.

Large 15" swordfish,
$110.00 – 135.00.

Deco swordfish with
Fiberglas shade,
$95.00 – 110.00.

Plaster squirrel with Fiberglas clamp-on shade and small pinholder, 3-way light, $65.00 – 80.00.

Blue-green fish with paper shade, $85.00 – 110.00.

Swordfish with brass base holder, $75.00 – 90.00.

Miscellaneous

Ceramic flamingos with airbrushed decoration, $85.00 – 100.00.

Ceramic basket with bulb inside, $45.00 – 55.00.

Ceramic basket with light inside, $50.00 – 60.00.

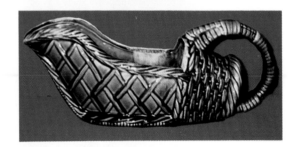

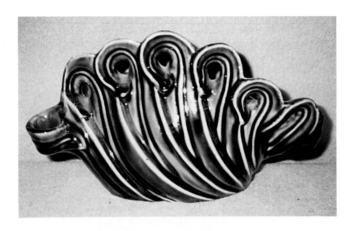

Green form with planter, signed Genuine Sheridan China by Luminart, $65.00 – 80.00.

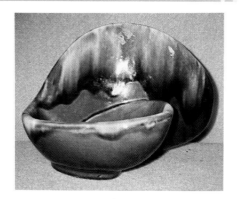

Ceramic light with planter,
$45.00 – 60.00.

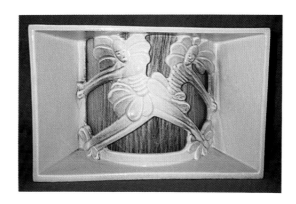

Deco dancers with Fiberglas shade, $85.00 – 110.00.

Ceramic shell with gold decoration, light inside makes top web glow, $85.00 – 95.00.

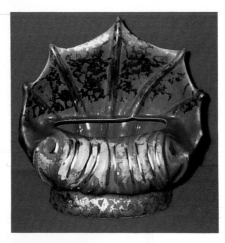

Pink and gold Aladdin's lamp, $60.00 – 75.00.

Paper fan with brass center, $45.00 – 60.00.

Double shell with light between two shells, $65.00 – 90.00.

Oak leaf with planter and Fiberglas decoration, $85.00 – 95.00.

Limb and leaf configu-
ration, $75.00 –
95.00.

Plaster lounge with "Fibrez" shade, $50.00 – 65.00.

Plaster leaf with airbrushed decoration, $55.00 – 75.00.

Ceramic base, Fiberglas body and shade, top removable, $75.00 – 85.00.

Double ceramic planter, brass base and Fiberglas shade, $65.00 – 85.00.

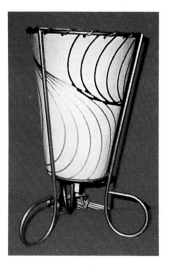

Fiberglas shade with brass base and holder, $35.00 – 50.00.

Fiberglas lamp with brass base, $55.00 – 60.00.

Fiberglas shade with brass holder, $35.00 – 50.00.

Hawaiian woman paddling canoe, gold fleck decoration with planter, $95.00 – 120.00.

Green foliage with planter, signed Genuine Sheridan China, By Luminart, $55.00 – 70.00.

Shells, plastic figures on plaster
bases, $50.00 – 65.00.

Shells, plastic fish on plaster
base, $50.00 – 65.00.

Shells, coral on plaster
base, $45.00 – 60.00.

Ceramic planter with Fiberglas shade and brass filigree holder, $75.00 – 100.00.

Ceramic shell, $75.00 – 90.00.

Shells, plastic figures on plaster base, $50.00 – 65.00.

Vases with bulb inside, light comes through slits on side, $55.00 – 85.00 each.

Maroon flower with planter, $55.00 – 70.00.

Gold flecked leaves and fruit with planter, $55.00 – 70.00.

Pot metal musicians with frosted globe, $120.00 – 135.00.

Seated Pan, light comes through holes to light up figure, $85.00 – 110.00.

Soapstone "Tower of Pisa" with light inside, windows light up, $135.00 – 145.00.

Ceramic with Fiberglas shade and original flowers, $75.00 – 100.00.

Paper, wood base and brass lighted scene, signed Helm-scene, Grand Rapids, Mich., $100.00 – 120.00.

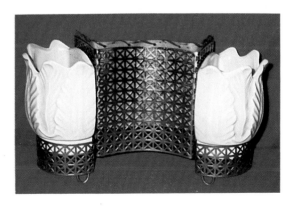

Double flower planters, brass with Fiberglas fitted shade, $95.00 – 110.00.

White metal motion lamp with reverse painting on glass, inside metal revolving cylinder causes look of moving waterfall, National Company, $225.00 – 275.00.

Glass, brass and plastic with original flowers and brass base, $55.00 – 65.00.

Plaster well with green satin globe, $90.00 – 120.00.

Brown branches, $55.00 – 75.00.

Ceramic flower with light inside, $70.00 – 90.00.

Flower with light inside, signed ESGO Light Corp., L. A. 15, Calif., $55.00 – 60.00.

Metal venetian blind-type shade with wooden base and sides, $95.00 – 120.00.

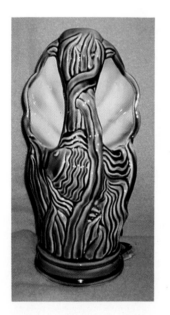 

Ceramic shell and seaweed with light inside, interesting back, signed Luminart, Sheridan China, $120.00 – 145.00.

Small 8" flower, $60.00 – 85.00.

Flower, leaf, shell arrangement with light inside, signed Italy, $65.00 – 85.00.

Ceramic shell with applied flowers, $85.00 – 100.00.

Ceramic base, brass ring and Fiberglas shade, $55.00 – 70.00.

Large 18" leaf, $85.00 – 95.00.

Ceramic with light inside, $50.00 – 70.00.

Planter with brass base, $35.00 – 45.00.

Planter with brass holder, $35.00 – 45.00.

Ceramic violin, signed Lane, $95.00 – 110.00.

Ceramic planter with brass base, $35.00 – 45.00.

Plaster feathers, signed F.A.I.P., $75.00 – 90.00.

Planter with brass holder, $30.00 – 45.00.

Planter and light, 8", $35.00 – 45.00.

Double ceramic ladies on wooden base and brass filigree, Fiberglas shades, $95.00 – 125.00.

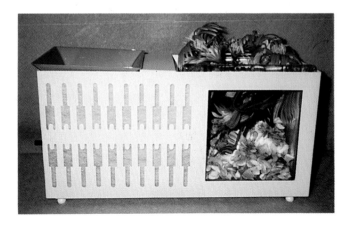

Metal planter, glass aquarium, with original flowers and gravel, $85.00 – 95.00.

Multi-color leaf, airbrushed decoration, signed Lane & Co., 1958, $85.00 – 95.00.

Glass block with original flowers, wooden base, light inside, $82.50 – 95.00.

Shell-like ceramic, $55.00 – 75.00.

Small bisque boat and figures with frosted glass shade, $75.00 – 95.00.

Brass filigree lamp with planter and Fiberglas shade, $75.00 – 85.00.

Pink ceramic flower with light inside, $80.00 – 110.00.

Large ceramic flower with light inside, $75.00 – 90.00.

Near-porcelain lighthouse with light inside, signed Made in California, $110.00 – 125.00.

Ceramic religious light with 3D-look plastic front, $110.00 – 125.00.

Brown grain mill with lighted window and planter, $75.00 – 95.00.

About the Author

Tom Santiso is in his fifth and he says hopefully his last career. He has been a high school math teacher, a "One-Man-Band" musician, auctioneer, antique dealer, and with this book, an author.

He has a masters degree in mathematics from the University of New Hampshire and taught math for 20 years in Pennsylvania and New Jersey. As a musician he wrote and released five singles.

For the past 10 years he has been a working auctioneer doing mostly good estates when they come along. He currently belongs to the Hawley Antique Exchange Co-op in Hawley, Pennsylvania.

Out of the many collecting phases he has gone through, his latest and most extensive, TV lamps, prompted him to write a book and price guide on the subject. There have been other books that included TV lamps of the 1950s, however, this book will raise the whole lot of these "forgotten lamps" to their own collecting level.

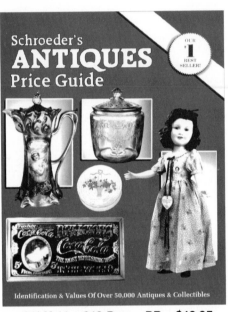